Letters to Mum

Letters to mum

Selected from a competition by
Mother magazine and Buzby Club

With illustrations by
Nigel Alexander

ARROW BOOKS

Arrow Books Limited
17-21 Conway Street, London W1P 6JD

An imprint of the Hutchinson Publishing Group

London Melbourne Sydney Auckland
Johannesburg and agencies throughout
the world

First published 1984
Reprinted 1984

© ipc magazines 1984

Illustrations © Nigel Alexander 1984

Set in Lectura by Photobooks (Bristol) Ltd.

Made and printed in Great Britain
by Anchor Brendon Limited, Tiptree, Essex

ISBN 0 09 933400 3

Introduction

Towards the end of 1982, *Mother* magazine and British Telecom's Buzby Club for young children got together to stage a letter-writing competition. Letters had to be written by children, under 15 years of age, to their mothers about the relationship between them.

There were 27 prize winners in all across the various age groups, and the judges had an unbelievably difficult job, which is why we on *Mother* are so delighted that this book allows many more from the hundreds of letters entered in the competition to be made available to a wider audience.

Children really do have a delightful way with words and we felt you would enjoy reading the letters 'warts and all', complete with mis-spellings and their version of punctuation – or lack of it!

One of *Mother* magazine's most popular regular features is on the last page of each issue – in fact, for many regular readers it's last page first, to see if they have made it into print that month. 'Last Word', as the page is called, is a monthly compilation of the things young children say as they acquire language and learn more about the world around them. This is truly a thrilling world where a new moon is called a big toe nail, walking through autumn leaves is like eating burnt toast and ravioli are sausages in tea bags. Anyone with children – or related to them – can probably supply a year's worth of 'Last Word' for us. I know my own daughter who is 3½ years old delights me daily with her sayings.

The best discovery of all about the letter-writing competition was that the originality of pre-writing years is not lost, and children still come out with things that not only strike a chord in their own mothers but that can be enjoyed and appreciated by people of all ages who will delight in the innocent, unique frankness of children.

Buzby is very much an invention of the telephone age, but the art of letter writing will certainly not be lost by the next generation if the contributors to this book are anything to go by.

Editor, *Mother* magazine

Dear mummy
the thingS I like about you
most are you Lett Me Keep a
Stray Kitten Wheen I had
already got a dog called DJoius
a FiSH colled Dublin and a
catterpillar called Tim and you
did not Say She is going even
wHen She Weed in the ivy
Plant
Love
Felicity

Felicity Gaizely, age 5
FIRST PRIZE WINNER

Dear Mum,

This is what I think of you. I think you are a very nice mum. but sometimes you get on my nerves, what I mean is, is that when I'm helping to do the chores and I look out the window and see it is raining and you have been planning to go out, I tell you its raining and you'll start singing Shakin' Stevens song of 'its raining in my heart'. I think you are hilarious sometimes. when you did not know you were still ng your slippers and you were going ing, I only just stopped you when you g g down the path. I'm glad she thought it was funny because its nice to have a sense of humour.

I wouldn't like to have a mum with no sense of humour, and who was serious all the time. Of course, she isn't funny all the time, she is serious when she has to be. If she was serious all the time it would be terribly boring for everyone. My mum is very nice and I wouldn't want any other.

Penelope Buckland, age 12

Dear Mum
    This is how I feel about you. You are extremely kind like last week you gave me 50p, you are concerned about my schoolwork and where I play.

However when my teeth fall out you accuse me of kissing the girls and that bugs me! But I love you any way.

    from Paul

Paul Connor, age 8
FIRST PRIZE WINNER

Dear
       Mum,
This is how I feel about you.
You are really such a good sort.
You have your ups and downs
in life but it doesn't matter.
Because I like you all the same.
I Wish there were more of you
about

              bye

Richard Smith, age 9

Dear Mum this is how I feel
About you you are such a
wonderfull mum sometimes But
you can Be such A Bore at
times and your always telling
me oFF. Please stop not letting
me watch the coloured televisen
and when ever I want to watch
someting saying Black & white
televisen! it annoys me so much

Armelle Ellison, age 8

Dear mum
This is how I feel about you.

I love you mum but why do you say
Time for bed when I want to play?
When I fancy fish fingers to eat
Why do I get a plate of mince meat?
I know it's only for my good
But why must I do the things I should?

Catherine Rendell, age 9

Dear Mum,
     This is how I feel about
you. I think you are the most
important in the whole world.
Daddy makes me laugh but you
are the One who does all the
cleaning, cooking and worring
about me.

There is one thing i do not like.
You talk too much.

          Love
          Lindsay ××

Lindsay Heyes, age 8
RUNNER-UP

Dear mummy

the things I like about you most
are your furry nose and you let
me sleep with you and look
after me when I am poorly and
let me make Cakes and buy me
presents. and clothes and taka
me to nice places and to see my
awtys and cousins and the
puppy and the hen's and buy
me yoyo Pisca tey

Love Kay

Kay Perry, age 6

Dear mummy,

the things I like about you most
are you make good food, you
buy good drinKs and you are
cuddLy.

I like it when you tuk me in at
night and when you read to me
and when you play with me

Love from Russell

Russell Millard, age 6

Dear mummy the things I like about you most are my little cute hamster and it is white that you bought me and I like it when you chuk me on my bed and tickle me and I laugh and I like you putting a pony tail in my hair

Rachel Brown, age 5

Dear MuMMy the things I Like
about you most are the cuddles
you give me and how warm you
feel HoW When i am ill you
find games to play when I have
to use my breathing machine
and best of all For growing
baby Katie in Your tummy

Michelle ×××××

Michelle Smith, age 5
SECOND PRIZE WINNER

Dear mummy the things I like
about you are. You come to
meet me at school and,
sometimes take me to the park.
You make things with me. You
wear LoveLy dresses. You are
the best Mum in the world.
Thank you.

Wendy Pitt, age 6

dear mummy the things that I
like about you most are your
hands because of the ring

I like you reading me stories
With lots of love from Helen

Helen Chayer, age 5

Dear Mum,
      This is how I feel about
you. . . .

Sometimes you annoy me in the
way you talk to my baby sister
in a silly voice, or nag about me
not doing od a jobs around the
house, but you are
understanding, generous and a
very good sport. So thanks
Mum.

Francine Howell, age 13

Dear Mummy
the things I like about you most Are

Wen She Kind
Wen She very nis
Wen She nis
Wen she helps Me
Wen She Lets Me Wach top and the Pops
Wen she Buy Me Swees
Wen She Buy Me Books
and Wen She Buy Me a Birthday Present
I lick her in pretty clothes
I lick her Wen she Buys me new xlothes
I lick her Wen she reds Me a StorIES
and give Me cuddles

I Love You lots Mummy

Love
Charlotte

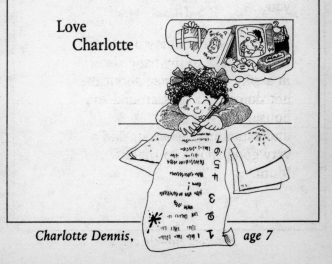

Charlotte Dennis, age 7

Dear
   Mum this is how I feel
about you I am sorry when I
upset you. I dont take a acount
of what yove done for me, I
havent thought of how yove
always been there to help me
when I was ill and all that
       Love
          Richard
       P S Thank - you

Richard Thackeray, age 12

Dear Mummy
    The things I like most
about you are firstly you buy
me food and clothes. You care
for me. You help me at
crosswords and lots of other
things. You say Prayers with
me. Sometimes you bring me to
exciting places and every week
you buy me a lolly.

Love Roderick

Roderick Kenny, age 6

Dear mummy, the things I like
about yoy most are you are.
Soft and you have a red nose
and I like my mummy when she
has eye shadow on. from Helen

Helen Munro, age 5

Dear Mum,
    This is how I feel about
you. . .
You are the very nicest mum I
know, and not too fussy like
some are. You are very kind,
and always ready to help others.
For being so super you ought to
have a badge saying:-

NEVER FEAR,
FOR CAPABLE ME
IS HERE!

Frances Garland, age 12

Dear Mum

This is how i feel about you sometimes
your nice and sometimes your angry
but most of the time your quite nice.
When you get angry with me you send
me up to my room. In the morning you
wake me up and i get angry
with you because i feel tired.
When I want some thing you to buy
me and you say no i get angry with you
and don't talk to you for the rest of the
    day.
But most of the time your quite nice
to me and i am very lucking to hav a mum.

Shovon Islam, age 10

Dear mum,

This is How I feel about you I
think you are a good cook
especcially your Macarioni cheese
yum yum. But you always put
me to bed early when Im not
tired, and in the morning you
wake me up when i'm tired.
                    mum
                 is
                         tops

Claire Stuart, age 8

Dear Mummy the things I like
about you most are your
hairstyle clothes looking after
me. doing this for me when I
am poorly. cooking and shopping
for me. taking me from school.
taking me to shows swiming
and to the park. going on
holiday.

I love you Mummy. Emma

Emma Triffitt, age 6

DEAR MUM

I AM WRITING TO SAY I AM
SORRY THAT I PUT MY
FISHING MAGGOTS IN THE
FRIDGE IT WAS AMUSEING
TO SEE DADS FACE WHEN I
ASKED IF IT IS ALRIGHT TO
HAVE THEM IN THERE BUT
FOR ALL THAT I STILL LOVE
YOU HOPEING YOU WILL
STILL GIVE ME MY
SPENDING MONEY

YOUR LOVING SON
MICHEAL

Michael Williams, age 11
RUNNER-UP

Dear Mum,

this is how I feel about you. I think that you are the best mum in the world because you go to work and then look after my two brothers and me. I think that you should get an award for being so hard working.

Lisa Fish, age 12

Dear Mum,

ThiS iS how I feel about you. I'm very lucky to haVe Such a Kind mum. Every day you do everything to make me happy.

Quite often I'm grumpy. I do not like Sloppy KiSSing or girlS but I loVe my mum.

Good luck with your next diet.

Jonathan

Jonathan Cale, age 8
RUNNER-UP

Dear Mum,
     this is how I feel about
you. I like the way you buy us
treats sometimes. Its nice when
you let me stay up late. I am
pleased when you let me make
the dinner and when you make
some cakes.

I don't like it when you switch
off a programme that I want to
watch.

     Love
          from
               Stephen.

Stephen Robinson, age 10

Dear mummy,
The things I like about you most are when you are nice to me Because I Know that when you smack me you do'nt really mean it and you give me pocket-money and sweets and I Am sorey when I Am naughty

All my Love
Melanie

Melanie Charlesworth, age 6

Dear Mummy,
This is how I feel about you. I think you are very special by managing since Daddy left. Like woodwork and digging the garden. Although you don't earn much you still kept your promise about a birthday party.
Sometimes you get grumpy but I Love your cuddles.

Love, Miranda

Miranda Holmes, age 9

Dear mum
   This is how I feel about you . . . .

   You are a super mum and you let me have most things I wish for. You allow me to watch my favourite programmes on television but please please! stop giving me sausages for my breakfast.

Victoria Clements, age 11

Dear mummy,
   The things
      I like about you most are you are nice and you help me with my spellings you are always there when I need you when I am unhappy or feel scared you always take me to nice places if you have enough pennies

love
   from
      Zoe

Zoe Ambrose, age 6

Dear mummy, the things I like about you are letting me watch television and letting me go and Play with my friends and giving me money. I don't like going shopping with you Because you take me in too many shops. I don't like going to have a haircut.

love James

James Sreeves, age 7

Dear Mummy,

    the things I like about you
most are you and I have lots of
love to share. You are always
there When I need you. Its nice
to have someone to belong to
but even better having you
belong to me. You understand
my mistakes but quickly forget
them.
Cuddly Mummy. I dearly love
you.

Sarah

Sarah Walters, age 6

Dear Mum,
    This is how I feel about you.
You give me treats and lots to eat;
you're quite good-looking, but best at cooking.
You scrub and clean our little house,
are kind to Haffertee, my pet mouse.
You stop the squabbling with my brother.
There is no other like my mother.

Love,
Lois

Lois Owen, age 8

Dear Mummy,

The things I like about You are
that you cuddle and KiSS me.
The things I hate about you, are
that I always have to go to bed
early at night. Also you only
give me 15p when we go to a
jumble Sale

love Rachel

Rachel Lutz, age 6

Dear Mum,
    This is how I feel about
you. You are a very nice mum,
Except when you are in a bad
temper, and you smack me and
shout at me.

I like it when you are in a good
temper, and you are the kind of
mum I want.

        Love Sharon.

Sharon De'ath, age 10

Dear mummy

This is how I feel about you. I love you very much especially when you take me to the park and buy me ice-creams. sometimes you shout at me when I am naughty then I go off you a little bit. I hope you love me very much.

Andrew Balderston, age 8

Dear Mum, this is how I feel about you . . .

I love it when you're cheerful in the morning when everyone else is bad - tempered and grumpy, especially when I want to buy something you think I don't need you tell me I can't buy it, <u>afterwards</u> I'm glad I've got the money instead.
In short
MUM'S
RULE,
OK?

Kerrie Davies, age 13

Dear Mum

This is how I feel
about you I love you
because you play with
me. When I'am ill you
look after me you let
me go too bed late
sometimes. when you think
I am asleep you sneak
in and give me an extra kiss.

Love
Carey

Carey Nix, age 8

Dear mummy

the things I
like about you
are the way
you feel like a
nice warm bath
and your smiling eyes.

love Matthew

Matthew Evans, age 5

Dear Mummy,
    The things I like about you
most are that you cook for me,
love me, help me, do my hair,
read to me, let me get
"Buttons", help me read the
bible, give me surprises, give me
sweets, let me go to school, and
you have got glasses.

Love
from
Joanne.

Joanne Geddes, age 7

Dear Mum,

This is how I feel about you,
You make us laugh quite alot.

When we go out you see friends
and start nattering. When
television's on you natter. You
even natter to yourself.

I don't like you Vegatarian
cooking, I much prefer licking
out your sticky fatty bowls.

Love
Amanda
 ✗✗✗

Amanda Christy, age 11
RUNNER-UP

Dear mummy the things
I like about you most
are you give me
good par ties,
you play and
read to us all
the time and you
make me laugh
when you try to
park our car
you make loVelY meals
and I Love You
because you've a smiling
Face.

Laura Heyes, age 5

Dear mummy

The the things I like about you are your lovely barbacue spare ribs. I like your fat tummy because there is a baby in it. When you went to Mallorca I wrote I miss you very much I am looking forward for you coming home.

Love Richie ✕✕✕

Richie MacKay, age 7
RUNNER-UP

Dear mum,

    this is how I feel about
you. I think you're a wonderful
mum and do things with me
lots of other mums wouldn't.
You also have a lot of patience
you've given me a piece of
garden which you spend alot of
time helping me with.

with
    Love
        Catherine

Catherine Rolls, age 11

Dear Mum,
This is how I feel about you. . .

Even though we argue I love you and I know you love me too.

I do realise that you are moaning at me for my own good but I do not always think of this at the time.

Love
Teresa.

Teresa Howlett, age 13

Dear mummy,

The Things I like about you are that you are so kind, and though you are very poor and have to bring me and daniel up alone, you still Give us smashIing treats and lovely food. Thank you for beIng my mum. I love you very much.

Marc.

Marc Czarnocha, age 6

MUM, M for master chef
burnt, very burnt or charcoal
for dinner.
U for useless with a
washing machine. Best Jumper
streched, white school shirt is
pink going pinker.
The last M is for moaning.
It's her full time hobby.
Shes a mum in a million
no-one else can be so unlucky

from a fan of
your
Nigel Adames

Nigel Adames, age 13
FIRST PRIZE WINNER

Dear Mum
The things I like about you best are:- you are always there when I need you. you always welcome my friends around the house. you take my little dog for walks you work hard so we can go on exciting holidays you buy me nice fashionable clothes. I love you.

Lisa McNamee, age 12

Dear Mummy, the things I lick about you most are

1. you are loving and kind.
2. you are lovly and beautiful.
3. you look after me so Well.
4. you Buy me nice clothes.
5. you tatke me on lovely holidays
6. you cook nice dinners for me.
7. Because you are my mummy.

Rebecca Lunson, age 6

Dear Mum
    This is how I feel about you I think you are a SMASHING MOTHER! because you always help me with my homework and comfort me when I am not well.

You come to most of my Football matches and cheer me on. You hardly ever annoy me and you are kind to other people.

            Love from
            Carl.

Carl McCormick, age 10

Dear mummy,
the things I like about you
most are you are kind, becouse
you surprise me with treats.
you give me and Daddy loves
and cudles. you have got a bad
back but I still love you. you
make me yummy sausage and
mash and beans.

love from
Ashley

Ashley Pugh, age 7

Dear Mummy, The Things I
Like about you are: you do good
cooking and you Tell STories
about Major CHeese and Mrs
Weetabix you tidy up.

I Love you and you are funny.
and you are good at gardening.
you give me nice crisps for
break at SCHool and I like your
WHiStling.

Philippa Smith, age 6

Dear mummy

the things I like about you most
are when I see you when I come
out of school and when you let
me make jelly. I like to go
shopping as well with you and
sitting with you looking at
books I love you because you
are always there.

love Donna

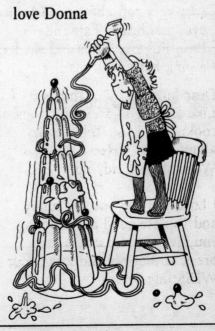

Donna Hopkins, age 5

Dear Mummy, the thing I like
about you when I am at a P.E.
Competition or at anything
Special. one time She bought an
Tiny Tears bath. And She has
very very soft cheeks and brown
eyes and brown hair and
beautiful eyes brow and she has
a pink hat with a feather

the end of my stiory

Susan Gillen, age 6

Dear mummy, the things I like about you most are doing dinner playing pairs, reading stories and Smiling

Shane Keeler, age 6

Dear Mum, this is how I feel about you. Sometimes I think you are very kind because you buy us things. You buy us the food to keep us alive. You take us to the Doctors when we are ill. You send us to bed when we should go.

Daniel Crautord, age 8

Dear Mum,
　　This is how I feel about
you;

O Mum, I love you dearly,
You are so very nice,
But when you start to shout at us,
We cower like little mice,

Oh how I like the cakes you bake,
There's nothing like a slice.

　　　I love you Mum!

Eric Morgan, age 10

Dear Mum
   This is how I feel about
you you are very kind and also
you are very beautiful. Theres
just one or two things you are a
bit overweight plus your cooking
is not that brilliant but, it is
edible. But please stop nagging
about my bedroom.

Matthew Patterson, age 10
FIRST PRIZE WINNER

Dear Mum, this is how I feel a bought you I like you beaucase you don't shout very much you also do not make me go to bed at the exact time

from
Christopher

Christopher Hipkins, age 9

Dear mummy,

the things I like about you most
  are.
Your food.
Shinyhair.
I love your face.
holding your hand.
You are kind
I like everything

love ✕ Sarah
✕✕✕✕✕✕✕✕✕✕ ✕✕✕✕✕✕✕✕✕✕✕

Sarah Smith, age 5

Dear mum,
This is how I feel about you. .

I think you are very comforting and clever because you own and work in a shop. You also let me purchase most of the things I want. Of course you have your faults! you moan to much.

Sonal Patel, age 12

Dear Mum,
   this is how I feel about you, you're very nice, I like you especially when you buy me new books and felt tips. I like you when you take me shopping. You are not so nice when you give me spaggetti and mince. But you're lovely otherwise.

Anthea Harris, age 10

Dear Mummy

the things I like about You are When You cuddle me because it feels nice and When Youre silly because its funny and doing things With You like reading stories or going out or making cakes and Warming My feet on You in bed Love from Amy XX

Amy Potter, age 5
RUNNER-UP

Dear mummy
    the things I Like about
you, you always cheer me up
when I am crying, and then I
end up laughing, you always
clean my mess up But you get
upset, you smack my Bum for
what I,v done and, then I get a
Big Sum

                    But Love
                        you mum

John Edden, age 5

Dear Mum,

    this is how I feel about you. you're wonderful because (yoy) you generously devote your time to looking after us, making things and baking.

    You fuss too much telling me to go to bed early – after a late night telling me I look pale

          Really I love you very much,

              love
                Ruth.

Ruth Kilgarriff, age 11

Dear mummy the things I like about you are you buy me new shoes and I love you and you cook me nice dinners love from Jenny.

Jenny Hunt, age 5

Dear Mummy, the things I like about you are your smile, the cuddles and kisses when I go to bed. I like pinching your fat cheeks! I enjoy dancing to music with you, and also going swimming. I do not like your cooking When you use onions and peas!

Tamara Pande, age 6

My mum is nice
She gives me sweets
she cooks my meals
and She looks after me
My mum has nice hands
she takes me out Places
She takes me to the Park
She has got nice hair
mummy Plays nice games with me
I Love my Mummy Lots

Natalie Cummins, age 6

Dear Mum,
        this is how I feel about
you.
        I love you very much
with you'r smokey blue eyes,
and the white hairs that are
coming among the brown, but
you are a bit too fat.
        You have a funny sence
of hummer but you have a nice
smile

        Julian

Julian Wardle, age 12
RUNNER-UP

Dear Mum
    This is how I feel about
you. You're a kind Mum but
some things do annoy me, You
say to me,
                "Go and do your
homework" straight after school
when I have had a busy, tiring
day. But sometimes you're
much different and let me off
sometimes.

Love
    Nicola

Nicola Skilton, age 10

Dear Mum,
     This is how I feel about you.
     You are a very hard working Mum. You seem as if you never stop. One minute the vacuum cleaner is out, the next minute you're washing up.
     You are a very kind Mum and deserve alot of praise.

                    Yours truthfully,
                    Anthony.

Anthony Gant, age 12

Dear Mummy,

the things I like about you most
are you buy me Food to eat.
nurse me when I am ill. let me
help you shop and you buy me
toys.
　　you gave me a lovely home
and lovely baby brother. I love
you because you love me.

Lisa Browne, age 6

Dear Mum,
This is how I feel about
you! Ever since I had to stay
with my first dad I wanted you
because I was so badly treated.
I keept on dreaming that you
would have me to care for me
my dream came true. You are
the person who cares for me.
You are the most comforting
person when I am unhappy
my mum is so nice then. She is
a nice mum at all the time.
        Yours sincerly
                Tracon

Tracon Allen Lewis, age 12
SECOND PRIZE WINNER

My Mum is very unusal.
she looks ordinary, she has fair
hair blue eyes and she is five
foot nine inches tall. I think she
is very pretty. I know she is
kind and gentle most of the
time but no one really believes
me because she is a dentist.

James Buckley, age 10
RUNNER-UP

Dear Mum
    This is how I feel about you.

wont let me stay up at night
time to watch T.V. and when
you tell me off I think you are a
pain in the neck but on the hole
you are good mum let's me go
swimming also your food is
good.

Love stuart

Stuart Read, age 10

Dear mummy

The Things I
like abouT you
are
thaT you are
good to me
and my liTTle
broTher
and Nero The dog
and The cat and
our Ten hens. sumTimes you.
get a bit cross
when dad is on
The Oil rig but
you are OK after your coffee

Love Neil

Neil Moir, age 5

Dear Mum,

this is how I feel about you,
even though your far away, I
know you'll be home soon, but
It still isn't the same, because
there's something missing,
something only you can fill.

A hole that's in my heart.
A Jug with out water.
A heart with out Love.

Rachel Patey, age 15
RUNNER-UP

Dear Mummy the things I like about you are the way you play with me, You made me a skipping rope and learned me how to skip. Mammy I like you kissing me when I go to bed.

Shona Power, age 5

Dear mummy the things I like about you are, you tuck me in bed and put toothpaste on My toothbrush. and make My tea and take me to ridde My pony, and you are pretty and read me storys and let me stay up till 8 o-clock of 9 o-clock. And let me play with my friends like Vicky and Juilet.

Emily Holmes, age 7

Dear Mummy

The things I like about you are
bright smiling eyes like the
stars and the moon big cuddle
when you meet me from School

The secrets you tell me about
Christmas and elves the songs
that you sing with me every day

Love John

John Hughes, age 6

Dear Mummy
the things I like about you most are your face because it always Looks pleased to see me. You got me a little brother and sister to Play with. You let me try on your shoes You make nice chips and puddings

Love
Sharon
×××X

Sharon Summers, age 5
SECOND PRIZE WINNER

Dear Mum,

This is how I feel about you.

you are loving and give us loads
of treets. Somtimes you are in a
bad moode and swear alot.
When I come back from school
you are always there to greet
me. You cook everything that
we enjoy eating

Karen Mcguinness

Karen McGuinness, age 10

DEar Mummy

The things
I like about you most are tak ingmeto
Kenya. I like you r eyes. You let
Me have milk. You let me have
my pocket money and you have
nice clean teeth

Love from Joseph.

Joseph Chesters, age 6
RUNNER-UP

Dear Mummy

The things I like about you are
you take me to School every
day you always Play games with
me you cook nice food like
Shepherds pie and fiSh and
chips, and you watch telly with
me you Knit me jumpers.

Love
James

James Leal, age 6

Dear Mum
This is how I feel about you.

I think you are the most wonderful mother anyone could have. I am very sorry I have ever upset you, but you know the old saying "you always hurt the ones you love".

Your ever loving
daughter,
Clare

P.S. I love you.

Clare Gowrie, age 13
RUNNER-UP

Dear Mum

This is how I feel about you, especially your apple tarts, ... gorgeous . . . . . . but urrgh! chicken wings twice a week and why should it be my turn every Sunday morning to make the tea. Coming home from school your always there, you smile, and say, "homework first television after".

Love
Justin

Justin Marks, age 12

Dear mummy

The things I like about you
most are the baby in your
tummy

Love Caroline.

Caroline Helme, age 4

Dear Mum,

As I grown a little wiser, I'm beginning to realise why mentally handicapped children need extra love. Being jealous of my sister now seems silly. because I love her more too, as you have always done.

In a house of love everyone loves each other.

With Love

Guy Taylor, age 13
SECOND PRIZE WINNER

Dear Mum
    This is how I feel about
you I love haveing you waiting
to greet me when I come home
from school I love the Safe
feeling I get when were
together. you help me when I'm
hurt, without you our family
wouldn't exsist I love you mum

                    Anita ✗✗✗✗

Anita Smeeth, age 10

Dear Mummy The Things I like about you most are you give me spending money and Take me to gymnastics. you read me books in bed and cooks me nice cakes. I like going jogging with you but your a bit slow. And I love you very much. Love Hayley.

Hayley Calvert, age 7

Dear Mum,

This is how I feel about you. I am glad that you make me do my violin practice because it has made me good. I know that you love me and Richard so I am always happy to come home from school.

I will always love you.

Andrew

Andrew Asbury, age 8

Dear Mummy
    the things
        I like about you most are
How You Make jumpers Fro
instance I especially like a
jumper theat had Pandas on it
and I also like you tucking me
in at night time.

Love from   Sarah

Sarah Peall, age 6

Dear mum
    this is how I feel about
you, you've a kind heart and
always helpful. I'm sorry I fight
my brothers and sisters as I
know that we've lost Our baby
sister Kiki and with dad losing
his job. I don't mean to hurt
you.

Your
    Loving
        ZOE

Zoe Stroud, age 10

Dear Mummy,

        The things
I like most about you are:

You tickle me.
You get my meals.
You hug me.
You buy me things.
You love me.
You give me money.
I dont like you when you cut
my finger-nails!
        Now- no more! Yours
sincerely,
        Felicity McLean.

Felicity McLean, age 7

Dear Mummy,
        The things I like about you
are having crackers at Christmas
and pennies right through my
Birthday cake.

I like going into Mummy's bed
and getting a cuddle and my
Dad snores in Mummy's bed. I
like Mummy making hot
porridge before school.

Douglas Leishman, age 5
RUNNER-UP

Dear Mum,
      This is how I feel about
you. I think your wonderful
making beds breakfast and
doing the boring things. But is
what I dont like is that I have
to go to bed early. When I dont
eat my dinner Im forced to eat
it.

                  Love Nicholas

Nicholas Watkins, age 10

Dear mummy

The things I likeabout you are
the way you love me better
When I'm poorly. Sometimes
you upset me by shouting if I
am naughty (I suppose I deserve
it but I don't think that at the
time) but you are still the best
mom in the Whole World.

Karen Montgomery, age 7

Dear mummy,

This is how I feel about you, mostly you are like other mothers, and that is sometimes good and sometimes bad. The things I like most about you is that you buy chicken kiev, have my friends home from school to play and you take me on outings. The things I do not like about are that I have to go to bed early. I never see holiday on ice because I'm in bed.

You're loving daughter
Anna.

Anna Kilby, age 9

Dear Mummy,
    The things I like about you
ares the way you comfort me
and send me to sleep by
stroking my fringe you make
me laugh when you Open the
kitchen cupboard in the kitchen
and all the pans fall out and
you jump up and down and
scream.

Love Alexi ✕ ♡ ✕ ♡ ✕ ♡ ✕ ♡

Alexi Rea-Brown, age 7
FIRST PRIZE WINNER

Dear Mummy, the things I like about you are letting me have my choice of food, you promise to get me a piano and watches for my 7th and 12th birthday, you play karate with me sometimes and I wish God let you live for ever because I like you.

Adetilekia Binitie, age 6

Dear Mum,
    this is how I feel about
you. I feel your'e the dearest
person on earth. Who is caring,
understanding and loving.
When I act wrongly, I get
punished. But I know you know
best, and I'm sure you want me
to get the best out of life, and
your'e doing a jolly good job. I
Love You!

        Love Robert
          ×××

Robert Mitchell, age 13

Dear mummy

The things I like. a bout you
help me to read book. and to
read French words and you
make nice dinners like fish
fingers omelette and chips and
beef burgers you let me hold
the baby some times and letting
me push the baby a. long when
we go to shoping you buy me
nice books and colouring books.

Vaschil Rughoo, age 5

DEAR MUM

LET ME TELL you HOW I
FEEL ABOUT you I KNOW
LIFES NOT THAT EASY FOR
you BRINGING UP ME AND
MY SISTER ON YOUR OWN.
BUT I DO LOVE AND
APPRECIATE you EVEN
THOUGH I DONT ALLWAYS
SHOW IT ONE DAY I WILL
PAY YOU BACK.

DARREN

Darren Drape, age 13
RUNNER-UP

Dear Mum,

This is how I feel about you. You were right about 'Tiswas', it is a terrible programme. Now that I am older why can I not stay up later? I know you are old now and your hands are rough looking after us "twins" but I love you.

Andrew Leishman, age 9

Dear mummy the things I like about you are you got me a birthday cake for my 5th birthday.

My Mummy washed the car. My Mummy has been on My big sisters horse and she has been on bare-Back. My Mummy Bumped the car on a lamp-post. My Mummy got me a birthday cake for my 6th birthday

Avril McEwan, age 6

My letter

My mum laughs very loud.
she is some times slow at
getting jokes and likes Barry
Manilow. when in a bad mood
its best to do what she asks.
what I hates she is always
rushing me. I also wish she
would stop smoking but I love
her anyway.

Mark Ashworth, age 10
SECOND PRIZE WINNER

Dear Mummy the things I like about you are your cool and patient nature, your deep-hearted love and affection for me and your day to day caring that I wonder is there any other person in this world who can be so charming and smashing. May God bless you.

Kenward Gorg, age 7

Dear Mum

This is how I feel about you. Your very kind and thoughtfull, But when Me and My sister have arguments you always seem to blame me, and I feel very upset.

When it comes to buying Me something your very genarous, and you make me feel auful for Im spending your money and you make me comportable.

Pamela Craven, age 12
RUNNER-UP

Dear mummy the things I like about you are as pretty as a princess you are Kind and gentle you make super salads I Wish I could marry you mummy you cannot do sums you can sew you keep my hamster clean and give me bubble baths

Elton XXX

Elton Baddow, age 5

Dear Mum
    This is how I feel about you.

God must have a special magic when he put you together you are my friend, teacher, playmate, and because I am Disabled you are my Body you smooth all the aching in my Body. but you always make me laugh.

James Lake, age 12
FIRST PRIZE WINNER

Dear mummy the things I like about you most are

    When mummy gives me mealS and takeS me out to pantomines and Films and She takes me to the park When mummy is ill I miss about her doing meals becuse daddy hearly always makes omelettes

Julie Skurme, age 7

Dear Mummy,

the things I like best a bout you
are cuddles when you read me a
story and when you wrap me in
a towel after my bath. I like you
when you smile at me through
the railings when I come out of
school.

lots of love from

Louise

Louise Stone, age 5
RUNNER-UP